Math Expressions

Homework and Remembering • Volume 2

Developed by
The Children's Math Worlds Research Project

PROJECT DIRECTOR AND AUTHOR
Dr. Karen C. Fuson

This material is based upon work supported by the
National Science Foundation
under Grant Numbers
ESI-9816320, REC-9806020, and RED-935373.

Any opinions, findings, and conclusions, or recommendations expressed in this material
are those of the author and do not necessarily reflect the views of the National Science Foundation.

HOUGHTON MIFFLIN HARCOURT

Teacher Reviewers

Kindergarten
Patricia Stroh Sugiyama
Wilmette, Illinois

Barbara Wahle
Evanston, Illinois

Grade 1
Sandra Budson
Newton, Massachusetts

Janet Pecci
Chicago, Illinois

Megan Rees
Chicago, Illinois

Grade 2
Molly Dunn
Danvers, Massachusetts

Agnes Lesnick
Hillside, Illinois

Rita Soto
Chicago, Illinois

Grade 3
Jane Curran
Honesdale, Pennsylvania

Sandra Tucker
Chicago, Illinois

Grade 4
Sara Stoneberg Llibre
Chicago, Illinois

Sheri Roedel
Chicago, Illinois

Grade 5
Todd Atler
Chicago, Illinois

Leah Barry
Norfolk, Massachusetts

Special Thanks

Special thanks to the many teachers, students, parents, principals, writers, researchers, and work-study students who participated in the Children's Math Worlds Research Project over the years.

Credits

(t) © David Hancock/Alamy, (b) Kitch Bain/Alamy.

Illustrative art: Ginna Magee and Burgandy Beam/Wilkinson Studio; Geoff Smith, Tim Johnson
Technical art: Anthology, Inc.

Name _____

Homework

1. Make a table from the picture graph. Answer the questions.

Picture Graph

Ducks	🦆🦆🦆🦆🦆
Balls	⚽ ⚽ ⚽ ⚽
Kites	🪁 🪁 🪁 🪁 🪁 🪁

Table

Toys	Number

2. There are the fewest of which toy? _____

3. How many more kites are there than balls? _____

Answer the questions about the table below.

Beach Toys

Toys	Number
Buckets	12
Shovels	14
Beach Balls	7

4. How many more shovels are there than beach balls?

_____

5. How many fewer beach balls are there than buckets?

_____

6. There are the fewest of which beach toy?

_____

Name _____

Remembering

Use the graph to answer the questions.

Food at the Party

Sandwiches	🍔 🍔 🍔 🍔 🍔 🍔 🍔 🍔
Pizza Slices	🍕 🍕 🍕 🍕 🍕 🍕
Muffins	🧁 🧁 🧁 🧁 🧁

1. There are the most of which food? _____

2. There are the fewest of which food? _____

3. There are _____ more sandwiches than muffins.

4. There are _____ fewer pizza slices than sandwiches.

Add the numbers.

5. $7 + 10 =$ ☐   **6.** $35 + 8 =$ ☐   **7.** $63 + 20 =$ ☐

8. $56 + 2 =$ ☐   **9.** $77 + 4 =$ ☐   **10.** $34 + 60 =$ ☐

11. $73 + 7 =$ ☐   **12.** $84 + 9 =$ ☐   **13.** $29 + 30 =$ ☐

From Graphs to Tables

Name _____

Homework

Solve the story problems.
Use drawings and numbers.

---

1. Toby has 12 balloons.
Roberto has 5 balloons.
How many more balloons does
Toby have than Roberto?

_____
label

---

2. Nora has 4 candles on her
cake. Maria has 9 more
candles than Nora. How many
candles does Maria have?

_____
label

---

3. Meg bought 15 flags.
Alan has 6 fewer flags than
Meg. How many flags does
Alan have?

_____
label

Targeted Practice

Make a table from the graph.
Answer the questions.

Insects in the Garden

Bees	🐝🐝🐝🐝🐝
Ants	🐜🐜🐜🐜🐜🐜🐜🐜
Crickets	🦗🦗🦗🦗

Insects in the Garden

Insects	How Many

1. There are the fewest of which kind of insect? _____

2. How many more ants are there than bees? _____

Answer the questions about the table below.

Rides at the Fair

Rides	Number
Roller Coasters	7
Carousels	4
Trains	12

3. How many more trains are there than carousels?

   _____

4. How many fewer carousels are there than roller coasters?

   _____

5. There are the fewest of which kind of ride?

   _____

Comparison Story Problem Strategies

```
            ⌐- - - - - - - - - - - ¬
  |─────────┼─────────┼─────────┼─────────┼─────────┼─────────|
  0         1         2         3         4         5         6
  inches
```

1. How far did the little cricket jump? _____ inches

2. How far did the big cricket jump? _____ inches

3. How much farther did the big cricket jump
   than the little cricket? _____ inches

Solve the story problems.
Use drawings and numbers.

4. Ramzan's shoe is 6 inches
   long. His father's shoe is
   5 inches longer. How long is
   his father's shoe?

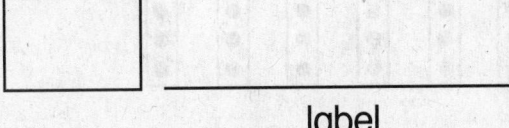

   label

---

5. Melissa caught a fish 12 inches
   long. Her sister caught a fish
   that was 4 inches shorter.
   How long was her sister's fish?

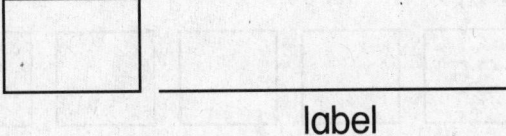

   label

Name Lauren

Remembering

Solve the story problem.
Use drawings and numbers.

1. Sonia saw 13 barns. Pedro
   saw 5 fewer barns than
   Sonia. How many barns did
   Pedro see?

_____ label

Write how many circles.

2.

How many?

3.

How many?

Write the misssing numbers.

4. | 35 | | | | 39 | | | | | |

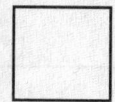
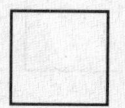
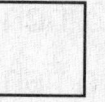
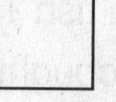
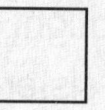
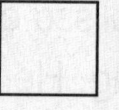

Measurement with Inches

Homework

Name _____

1. Measure the chains. Complete the table.

Paco's Chain

Leah's Chain

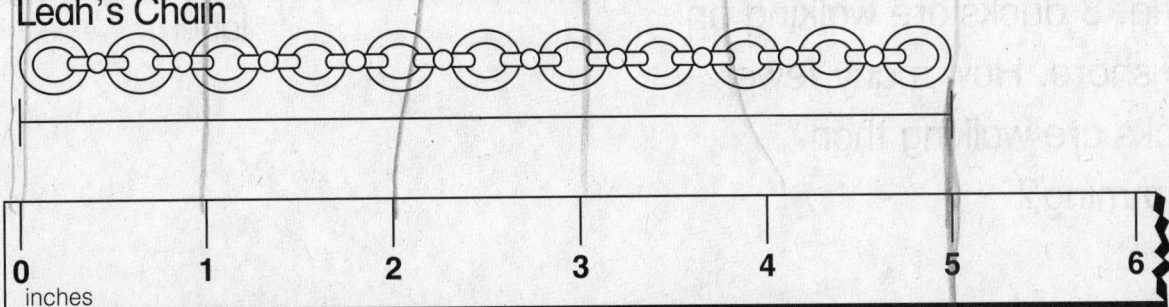

0 1 2 3 4 5 6
inches

Tara's Chain

Reed's Chain

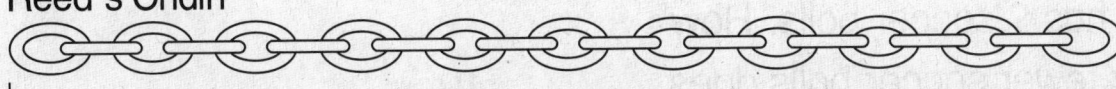

Chain	Length
Paco's Chain	
Leah's Chain	
Tara's Chain	
Reed's Chain	

2. How much shorter is Paco's chain than Leah's chain? _____

3. How much longer is Reed's chain than Tara's chain? _____

Targeted Practice

Solve the story problems.
Use drawings and numbers.

_____

1. 14 ducks are swimming in a
   pond. 8 ducks are walking on
   the shore. How many fewer
   ducks are walking than
   swimming?

   □ _____
   label

_____

2. Lynn's soccer team has
   13 soccer balls. Sue's soccer
   team has 9 soccer balls. How
   many fewer soccer balls does
   Sue's team have than Lynn's
   team?

   □ _____
   label

_____

3. Kim jumped 16 times with her
   jump rope. Evan jumped
   8 times with his jump rope.
   How many more times did
   Kim jump than Evan?

   □ _____
   label

Homework

Name _____

Ring half of the objects in each group.
Then fill in the blanks.

     Half of __6__ is __3__ .

1.    Half of ____ is ____ .

2.    Half of ____ is ____ .

3.    Half of ____ is ____ .

Solve the story problems.
Use drawings and numbers.

4. There were 12 pennies in my
   pocket yesterday.

   Now there are only half
   as many.

   How many pennies are
   there now?

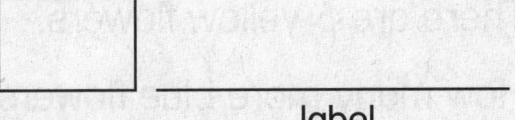
_____
label

5. There are 16 animals at the
   pet show.

   Half of them are dogs.

   How many dogs are there?

_____
label

Targeted Practice

Solve the story problems.
Use drawings and numbers.

_____

1. Leon has 9 shells.

Regina has 8 more shells
than Leon.

How many shells does
Regina have?

[   ] _____
        label

_____

2. There are 14 blue flowers in
the garden.

There are 6 yellow flowers.

How many more blue flowers
are there than yellow flowers?

[   ] _____
        label

_____

3. Justin traded 13 marbles.

Maria traded 4 fewer marbles
than Justin.

How many marbles did
Maria trade?

[   ] _____
        label

Hom eework

Name

Use the with numbers and with sticks and circles.

1. O

1. 37 + 45	2. 16 + 57
3. 25 + 39	4. 81 + 17

Solve the story problem.

Show your work. Use drawings, numbers, or words.

5. Yesterday, Rosa counted
   29 bikes. Today, she counted
   37 bikes. How many bikes
   did she count in all?

bike

☐ _____

label

Student Methods: 2-Digit Addition **229**

Targeted Practice

1. How many apples does Tom have?

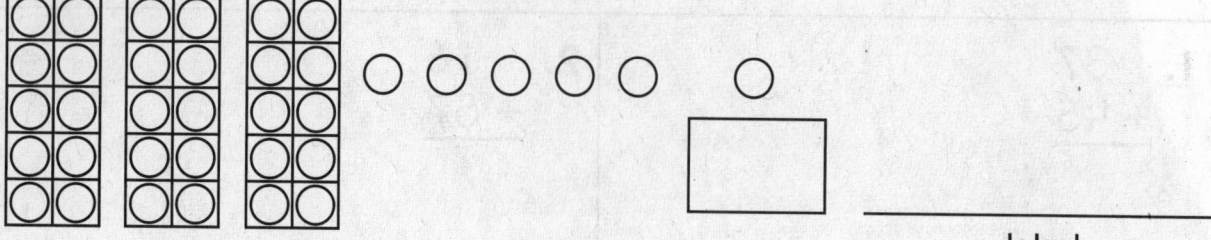

_____

label

2. How many apples does Bev have?

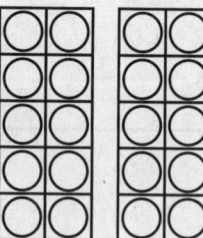 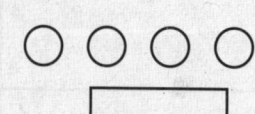

_____

label

3. How many apples do Tom and Bev have altogether?

Total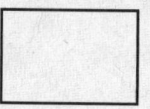

_____

label

_____

Solve with numbers and with sticks and circles.

4.   28
     + 45

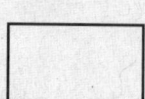

Total

_____

5.   54
     + 37

Total

_____

6.   69
     + 25

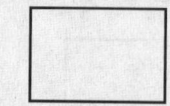

Total

Student Methods: 2-Digit Addition

Homework

Name _____

Add the numbers. Make a proof picture with sticks and circles.

1. 67 + 26	**2.** 32 + 37
3. 38 + 47	**4.** 53 + 39

5. How many nuts are there in all? Show your work.

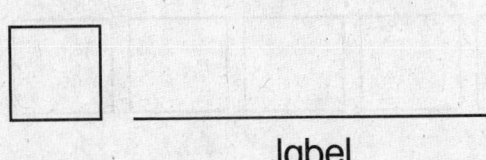

label

Remembering

Add or subtract.

1. $7 + 6 = \boxed{}$

2. $9 + 5 = \boxed{}$

3. $13 - 8 = \boxed{}$

4. $\boxed{} = 6 + 6$

5. $\boxed{} = 15 - 8$

6. $\boxed{} = 9 + 8$

Add the numbers.

7. $\begin{array}{r} 48 \\ + 20 \\ \hline \end{array}$

8. $\begin{array}{r} 64 \\ + 30 \\ \hline \end{array}$

9. $\begin{array}{r} 27 \\ + 50 \\ \hline \end{array}$

10. $\begin{array}{r} 19 \\ + 70 \\ \hline \end{array}$

11. Lucy had 9 pencils. Then she got 7 more pencils. How many pencils does she have in all?

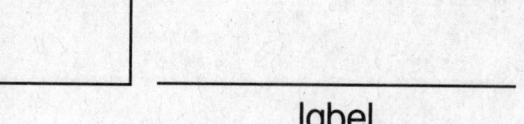

label

12. Continue the pattern.

5	10	15							

Addition of Tens and Ones

Name _____

Homework

Solve the story problems.

Show your work. Use drawings, numbers, or words.

1. There are 24 bikes behind the school and 19 bikes in front. What is the total number of bikes?

bike

[ ] _____
label

2. A quilt has 49 white pieces and 38 red pieces. How many pieces are there altogether?

quilt

[ ] _____
label

Add the numbers.

3. 68
 + 28

4. 49
 + 13

5. 72
 + 26

2-Digit Story Problems **237**

Name _____

Targeted Practice

Add the numbers. Did you make a new ten?

1. 56 + 28 New ten? yes ☐ no ☐	**2.** 29 + 37 New ten? yes ☐ no ☐
3. 42 + 19 New ten? yes ☐ no ☐	**4.** 74 + 25 New ten? yes ☐ no ☐
5. 47 + 27 New ten? yes ☐ no ☐	**6.** 13 + 54 New ten? yes ☐ no ☐
7. 65 + 32 New ten? yes ☐ no ☐	**8.** 69 + 23 New ten? yes ☐ no ☐

2-Digit Story Problems

Homework

Watermelon 58¢

Orange 39¢

1. Cesar bought a watermelon and an orange. How much did he spend?

[___] ¢

How many dimes? _____

How many nickels? _____

How many pennies? _____

Bananas 47¢

Lemons 28¢

2. Carla bought bananas and lemons. How much did she spend?

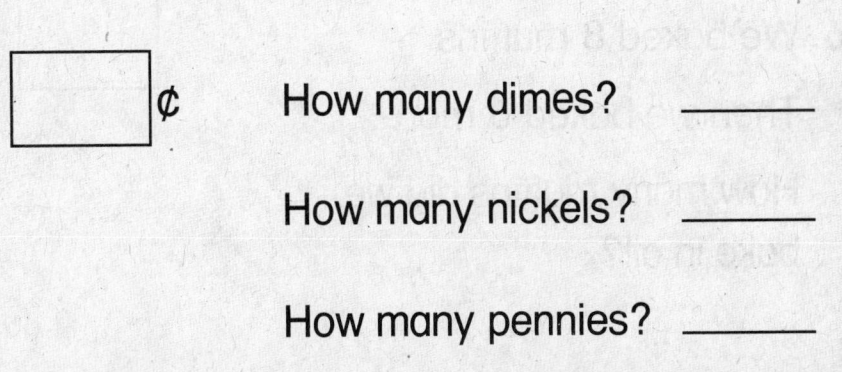

[___] ¢

How many dimes? _____

How many nickels? _____

How many pennies? _____

Remembering

Ring one fourth of the objects in each group.
Then fill in the blanks.

1.    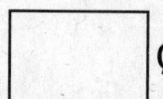 One fourth of ___ is ___.

2.     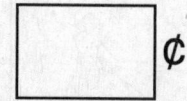 One fourth of ___ is ___.

3. ★★★★★★★★★★★★★★★★☆ One fourth of ___ is ___.

Count the money in each row.

4. [three quarters] ☐ ¢

5. [four quarters] ☐ ¢

Solve the story problem.
Use drawings and numbers.

6. We baked 8 muffins.

   Then we baked 6 more.

   How many muffins did we
   bake in all?

   ☐ _____
       label

Real-World Problems: 2-Digit Addition

Homework

Cut out the strips on the bottom of the page.
Use them to measure the trains.
Round up or down.

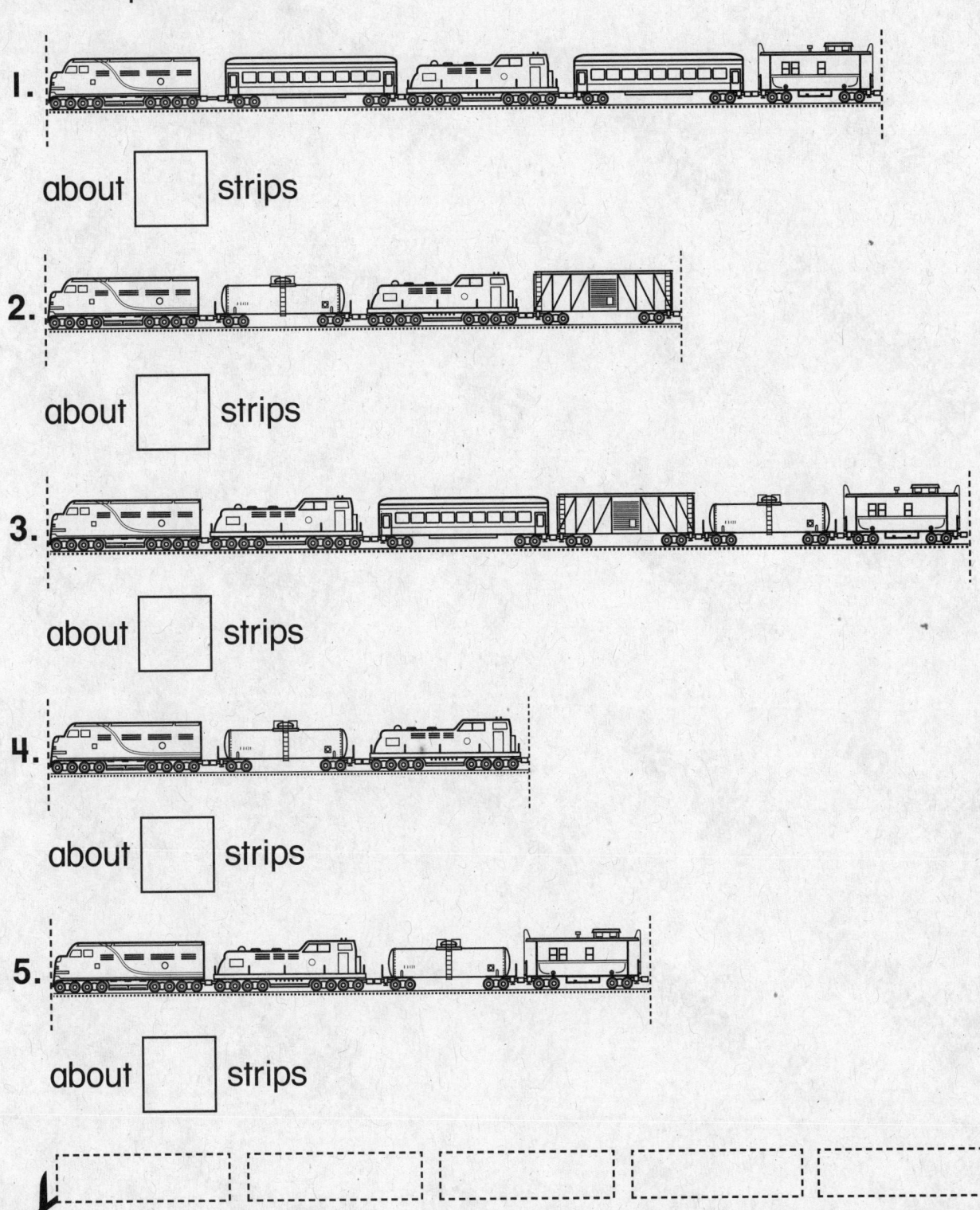

1.

about ⬜ strips

2.

about ⬜ strips

3.

about ⬜ strips

4.

about ⬜ strips

5.

about ⬜ strips

Measurement: Nonstandard Units and Rounding **273**

Practice

tory problems.

Show your work. Use drawings, numbers, or words.

e saw 30 sailboats,
oats, and 10 trains.
y boats did we see?

sailboat

_____
label

---

2. Mia has 28 white seashells, 26 grey rocks, and 25 pink seashells. How many seashells does Mia have?

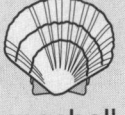
seashell

_____
label

---

3. On the farm, I saw 6 horses, 4 tractors, and 8 cows. How many farm animals did I see?

tractor

_____
label

➡ **4. On the Back** Write an addition story problem with extra information.

Solve the s

1. Today we
20 rowb
How mar

2. Mia has 24 white seashells.

3. Chris found a coral beside

Measurement: Nonstandard Units and Rounding

Name _____

Homework

Cut out the ruler or use your own ruler.

Measure some things at home.

Write the name of each thing. About how long is it?

1. I measured _____ .

It is about _____ inches long.

2. I measured _____ .

It is about _____ inches long.

3. I measured _____ .

It is about _____ inches long.

4. I measured _____ .

It is about _____ inches long.

5. I measured _____ .

It is about _____ inches long.

9

8

7

6

5

4

3

2

1

0

inches

Homework

Measure each piece of string to the nearest inch.

1. ～～～～～～～～ about ☐ in.

2. ～～～～～～～～～ about ☐ in.

3. ～～～～ about ☐ in.

4.　　　　　**5.**　　　　　**6.**

about ☐ in.

about ☐ in.

about ☐ in.

9
8
7
6
5
4
3
2
1
0

inches

Use an Inch Ruler

Name _____

Targeted Practice

Measure each piece of string to the nearest inch.

1. ∿∿∿∿∿∿∿∿∿ about ☐ in.

2. ∿∿∿∿∿∿∿∿∿∿∿∿ about ☐ in.

3. ∿∿∿∿∿ about ☐ in.

4.   5.   6.

about ☐ in.

about ☐ in.

about ☐ in.

9
8
7
6
5
4
3
2
1
0
inches

Name _____

Homework

Measure the sides of each gray shape with an inch ruler.

1.

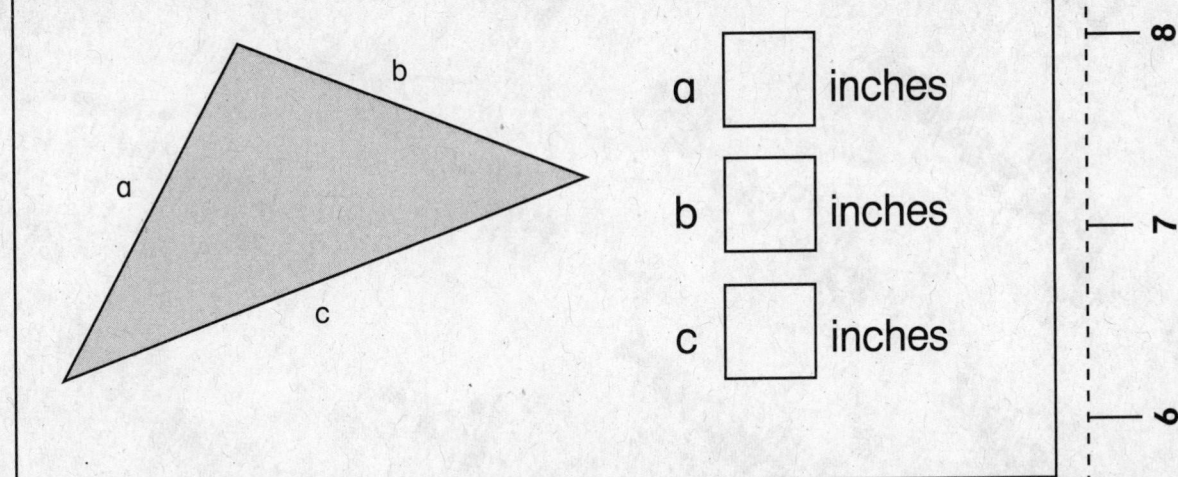

a ⬜ inches

b ⬜ inches

c ⬜ inches

2.

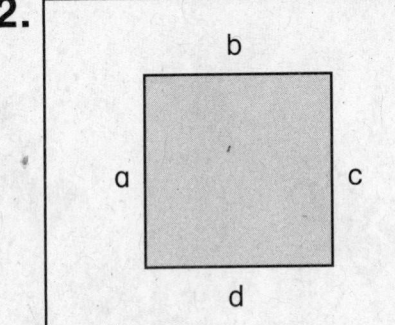

a ⬜ inch

b ⬜ inch

c ⬜ inch

d ⬜ inch

Square? _____

3.

a ⬜ inch

b ⬜ inches

c ⬜ inch

d ⬜ inches

Square? _____

9
8
7
6
5
4
3
2
1
0
inches

Measure Shapes in Inches **285**

Homework

Cut out the rulers. Measure the chains in
centimeters. Then measure them in inches.
Round the numbers. Fill in the table.

Chain	Centimeters	Inches
A	_____ cm	about _____ in.
B	_____ cm	about _____ in.
C	_____ cm	about _____ in.
D	_____ cm	about _____ in.

A

B

C

D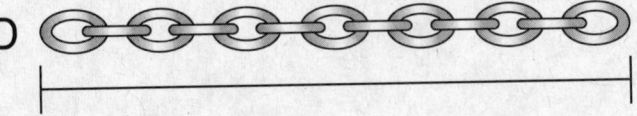

centimeters

─ 20
─ 19
─ 18
─ 17
─ 16
─ 15
─ 14
─ 13
─ 12
─ 11
─ 10
─ 9
─ 8
─ 7
─ 6
─ 5
─ 4
─ 3
─ 2
─ 1
─ 0

inches

─ 9
─ 8
─ 7
─ 6
─ 5
─ 4
─ 3
─ 2
─ 1
─ 0

Homework

1. Cut out the rulers. Measure some things at home. Round the numbers. Fill in the table below.

Object	Centimeters	Inches
Spoon		
Fork		
Toothbrush		

Solve the story problem.
Use drawings or numbers.

2. Lily has a ribbon that is 2 inches long. She has a string that is 9 inches long. How many inches longer is the string than the ribbon?

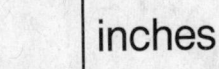
inches

20 19 18 17 16 15 14 13 12 11 10 9 8 7 6 5 4 3 2 1 0

centimeters

9 8 7 6 5 4 3 2 1 0

inches

Measure Shapes in Centimeters

Name _____

How far did each bug jump?

Measure in centimeters and inches.

Round the numbers. Fill in the table.

A ⊢————————————————————⊣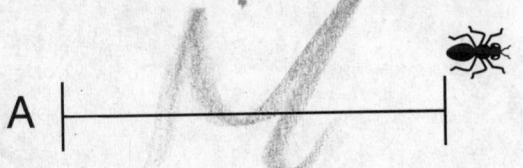

B ⊢————————————————————————————⊣

C ⊢————————————————————————————————⊣

D ⊢————————————————————————————————⊣

Bug	Centimeters	Inches
A	about _____ cm	about _____ in.
B	about _____ cm	about _____ in.
C	about _____ cm	about _____ in.
D	about _____ cm	about _____ in.

centimeters

20 19 18 17 16 15 14 13 12 11 10 9 8 7 6 5 4 3 2 1 0

inches

9 8 7 6 5 4 3 2 1 0

Homework

Ring the measuring tool you use.

1. How heavy?

 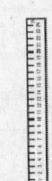 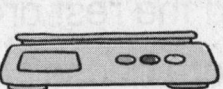 

2. How long?

  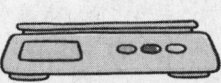 

3. How much it holds?

  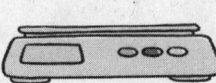 

4. How much it holds?

 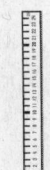 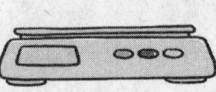 

5. How heavy?

 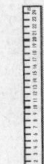 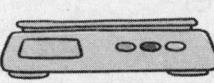 

Name _____

Targeted Practice

Solve the story problems.

Show your work. Use drawings, numbers, or words.

---

1. There are 16 birds in the yard. 9 are chickens, and the rest are geese. How many are geese?

goose

[ ] _____
       label

---

2. Lucie has 7 daisies and 9 daffodils. How many flowers does she have?

flower

[ ] _____
       label

---

3. I read 5 books this morning, and 8 more this afternoon. How many books did I read today?

book

[ ] _____
       label

---

4. Oliver saw 18 animals on his trip. 11 were moose. The rest were deer. How many were deer?

moose

[ ] _____
       label

Weight and Capacity